Easy Classic Favorites

TABLE OF CONTENTS

Stephens Development Company
distributed by

HAL•LEONARD®
CORPORATION
7777 W. BLUEMOUND RD. P.O. BOX 13819 MILWAUKEE, WI 53213

LARGO
from Xerxes

G. F. Händel

4

(LARGO)

(G. F. Händel)

ADAGIO CANTABILE
from Pathétique Sonata

L. v. Beethoven, Op. 13

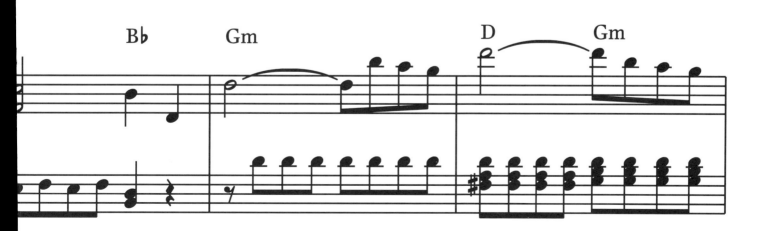

(ADAGIO CANTABILE)

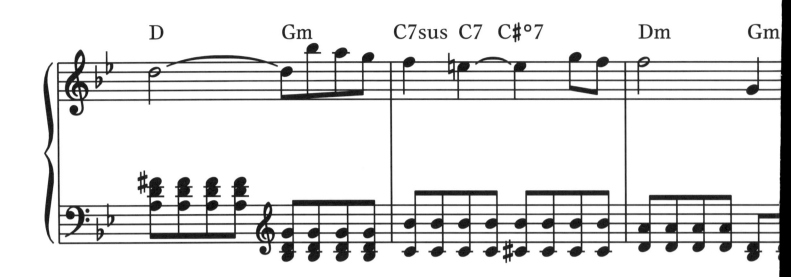

(L. v. Beethoven)

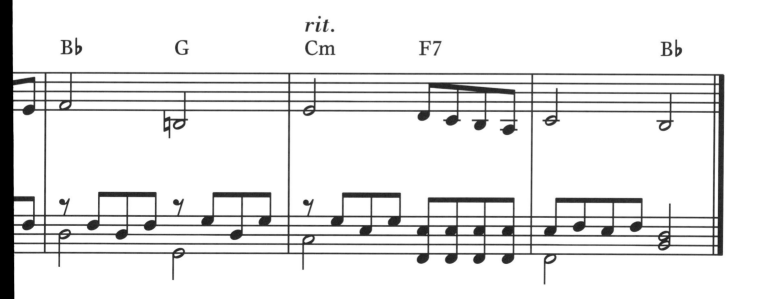

PIANO CONCERTO NO. 1
(Theme)

Andante

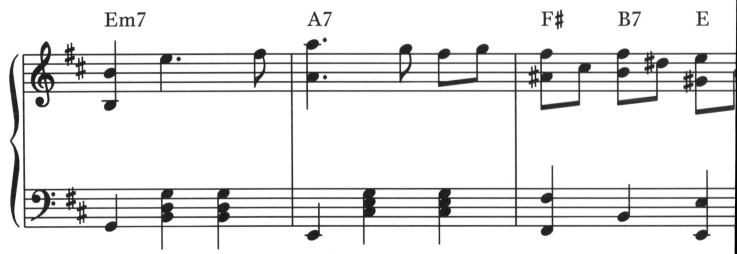

P. Tchaikovsky

(PIANO CONCERTO NO. 1)

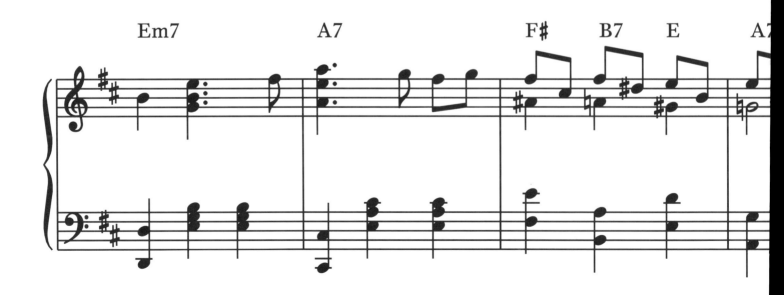

(P. Tchaikovsky)

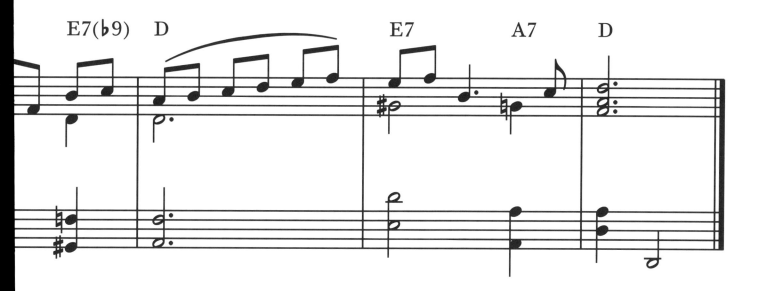

NOCTURNE

Andante

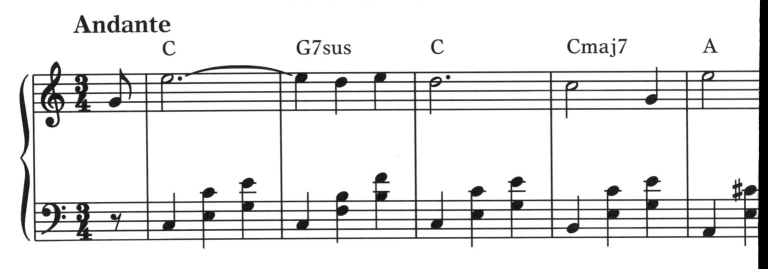

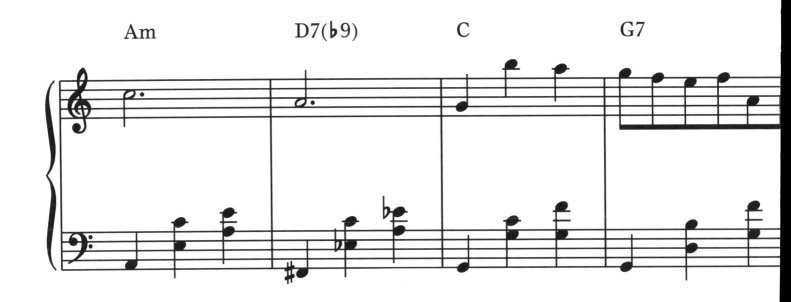

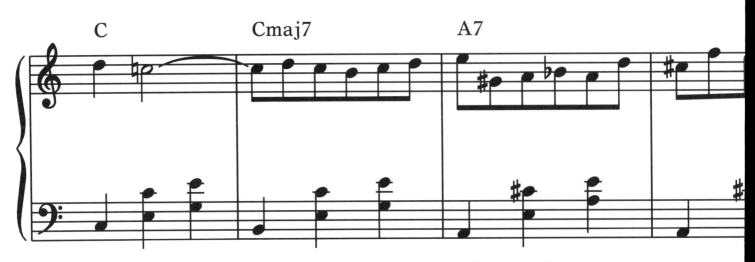

F. Chopin, Op. 9, No. 2

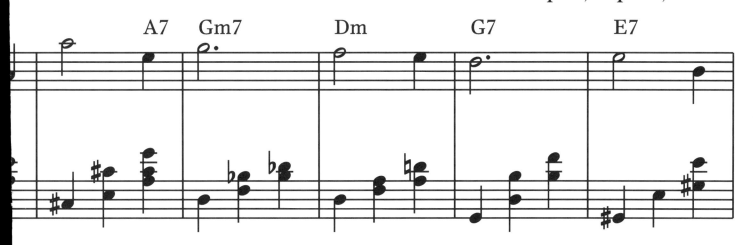

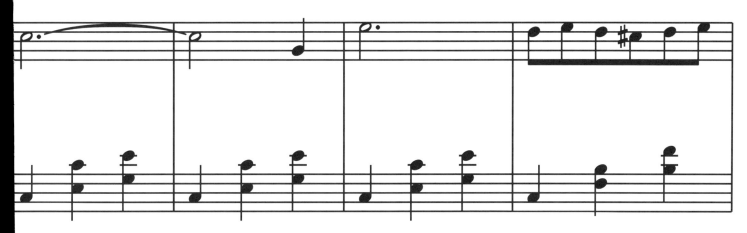

(NOCTURNE)

(F. Chopin)

PRELUDE

F. Chopin, Op. 28, No. 4

THE SWAN

Moderato and expressive

C. Saint-Saëns

(THE SWAN)

(C. Saint- Saëns)

LIEBESTRAUM NO. 3

Poco allegro, con affeto

F. Liszt

(LIEBESTRAUM NO. 3)

(F. Liszt)

INTERMEZZO
from Cavalleria Rusticana

Slowly and expressively

P. Mascagni